Published in the United States of America by Jennifer Abuzaina

Illustrations by Haya Kaabneh

ISBN: 978-0-578-99510-6

To my loving husband and children...

To the kind and generous people of Palestine...

I dedicate this book to you.

Let's Rhyme Through Palestine

Written by Jennifer Abuzaina

Illustrated by Haya Kaabneh

Marhaba! It's nice to meet you!

I hope you're doing fine.

My name is Amira from

Jericho, Palestine.

THE ARABIC NAME FOR JERICHO IS "ARIHA" WHICH MEANS FRAGRANT

Jericho The oldest City in The world

10.000 Years

HISHAM'S PALACE JERICHO, PALESTINE

It's the oldest city in the world

at 10,000 years old.

The weather is really hot,

the opposite of cold.

THE DEAD SEA IS EARTH'S LOWEST ELEVATION ON LAND

If you ever visit here,

there is a place you must see,

The lowest place on Earth,

It's called the Dead Sea.

It's not a sea like any other I must note,

There is so much salt in the water,

that you can float!

THE DEAD SEA IS 9 TIMES SALTIER THAN THE OCEAN

AL-MANARA SQUARE RAMALLAH, PALESTINE

If you go to the west,

Ramallah is where you'll be,

It's the busiest city in Palestine,

if you ask me.

Outside of the city there's many

groves of olive trees,

Relax in the shade

and feel a cool breeze.

PALESTINE HAS SOME OF THE WORLD'S OLDEST OLIVE TREES

DOME OF THE ROCK IS JERUSALEM'S MOST RECOGNIZABLE LANDMARK

The great city of Jerusalem

is next on our list.

The gold on the Dome of the Rock

cannot be missed.

Shop at the souk in the Old Town,

You'll find jewelry, souvenirs and

the traditional Palestinian gown.

SOUK IS THE ARABIC WORD FOR MARKET

THE SILVER STAR MARKS THE BIRTH SITE OF JESUS AT CHURCH OF NATIVITY

A town near Jerusalem,

Bethlehem by name,

The birthplace of Jesus

gave it its fame.

Manger Square has a church on the left,

a mosque to the right,

they coexist in peace;

they do not fight.

CHURCH OF NATIVITY AND MOSQUE OF OMAR BIN AL KHATTAB

THE OLD CITY OF HEBRON FEATURES NARROW STREETS AND BAZAARS

The village of Abraham,

Hebron as it's known,

The people are so friendly,

you will never feel alone.

They may offer you some

of their famous grapes,

And take you on a tour

of the beautiful landscapes.

OVER 25,000 TONS OF QUALITY GRAPES ARE PRODUCED ANNUALLY IN HEBRON

NABLUS IS FAMOUS FOR ITS SWEETS, OLIVE OIL SOAP AND BUSY MARKETS

Next is Nablus to our North,

I'm craving some kunafeh,

So let us set forth!

Made with pistachio, syrup and cheese,

This dessert will make you beg:

"MORE PLEASE!"

AL-AQSA SWEETS NABLUS, PALESTINE

FISHING IS A MAIN LIVELIHOOD FOR PALESTINIANS IN GAZA

Now we travel all the way to

Gaza City,

The view of the Mediterranean

is very pretty.

SAYYADIYEH IS A TASTY MIDDLE EASTERN FISH AND RICE DISH

You'll see many fishers fishing for fish,

So, families can gather and

enjoy the classic Sayyadiyeh dish.

Thanks for traveling through Palestine with me!

There's still very many places and sights to see.

Goodbye for now, I hope we meet another time.

To play, to learn and most importantly to rhyme.